REVELATIONS
OF
RELATIONSHIP

What You Don't Know About Finding
True Love and Sustaining Relationship

OLUWAFEMI "GFEM" OGUNJINMI

LIGHT SWITCH
P R E S S

Published by:
Light Switch Press
PO Box 272847
Fort Collins, CO 80527

Copyright © 2015

ISBN: 978-1-939828-28-6

Printed in the United States of America

CONTENTS

Praise.. I

Acknowledgement V

Foreword... VII

Foreword...IX

Introduction..XI

Communication...1

Transformational Approach to Dating 5

How to Stop Cheating....................................9

Love Makes You Blind, ...17

Marriage Restores Your Sight.......................17

Connection 21

Confusion of Women when Dating.................25

Persistent Character 29

Keys to Relationship Sustainability 33

Friend Zone...39

The Complement..43

Different Folks, Different Strokes 47

Family Time 51

Pick-up Line..55

Getting the Ring..59

Avoiding Basic Arguments with Your Wife.....................63

He's not interested..67

Questions and Answers 73

PRAISE

"Femi is the best at giving on target relationship advice without a lot of fluff. He'll tell you like it is and also help you to see the best solution for improving your relationship. You can't go wrong by checking out his book."

   - Michelle Barnum Smith,
     Dating & Personal Marketing Expert

"If you desire vibrant, authentic relationships, this book is for you. Femi codifies the qualities and characteristics of life-long, loving relationships."

   - Jeff Krantz, Author of Sales ROCKSTAR: How Top
     Producers Perform and Proud husband of 20 years to
     the April - the love of his life

"It gives me great pleasure to write an endorsement on this book, which was written by this spiritually inspired talented young man, Mr. Femi Ogunjinmi. When I read the first two chapters of this book, I saw truthfully that the spirit of God moves inside the author. Anyone that has the privilege to read this book will appreciate the power of the Holy Spirit. I highly recommend to everyone who wants to know spiritual facts concerning relationship in a practical and spiritual manner. This book gives in-depth of various challenges someone faces when in the process of finding a mate. It provides solutions to bridge the gap between secular relationship and biblical principles. It is my pleasure to tell you that this book is good. It is ideal for everyone to have and read. Most especially for Christians who are looking for ways and guide to strengthen their relationships. I therefore endorse and bless this book in the name of the Father and of the Son and of the Holy Spirit."

- Pastor Dr. Jerome Oyeneyin, The Light of Christ Church International. Dundalk, Maryland

'If you're having challenges in your relationship, read Femi's book. It has insights that have withstood the test of time."

- Elliott Katz, Author of Being the Strong Man A Woman Wants: Timeless wisdom on being a man

"Anyone who is searching for a life mate following biblical principles will find *Revelation of Relationship* by Femi Ogunjinmi to be the GPS navigational guide they've been searching for! *Revelation of Relationship* will not only provide the reader with a strategy to meet *the right person* but also offers insight into nurturing and maintaining that love for life."

- Kevin Darné, Author of *My Cat Won't Bark! (A Relationship Epiphany)*

"Femi takes the learnings of the Bible, traditional wisdom, and personal experience in helping others, combined with some down-home good sense and creates a book that reminds us that when our hearts and intentions are pure, we can find the right partner for life. High praise for an honest account of what it takes to find and keep a long-term loving relationship."

- Dr Wendy Williams, Author of The Globalisation of Love

"Revelations of Relationship reveals the writer's understanding of how to cultivate a delightful relationship. Gfem used his experiences as a good husband, respectable father, and a trainer of youth, a mass media guru and an obedient child of God to address issues and concerns about dating and the process of establishing a lasting relationship. His thoughts are based on Christian standards and time tested secular practices. The book is good for anyone that wants to do dating in a godly way, especially those who want to gain the confidence of their dates. Christian young-adults will specially benefit from the manner the writer presents "how to stop cheating." Christian ladies who want to consider biblical teachings relating to dating will find useful nuggets from this book. Gfem illustrates the importance of nonverbal communication in a manner that is thought provoking. You will agree with me that many relationships have been made or marred as a result of the orientation of the parties involved in the craft of nonverbal communication. Buy the truth! Get a copy of this book and take your relationship to the next level. Let me sound a note of warning! This book is stimulating. Once you pick it, you will want to read everything before you drop it. Make sure you have your highlighter by your side as you read this master piece. Finally, you can have a lasting relationship, however, with "WHO?" Where do you hang out? How are you perceived by the people around you? Out of all your friends, which one has the right character and positive influence? The book is an eye opener. Go and grab your copy."

> - Pastor Oladapo Oyewole, RCCG House of Praise Baltimore

"A must read masterpiece on sustainable relationship; a piece so cleverly written and lavishly loaded with insightful nuggets essential for meaningful, warm and impactful relationship; it will pass as a relationship manual in times to come.

> - Dr. Michael Fowowe, Pastor i/c RCCG Tabernacle of Praise, Edgewood, MD.

ACKNOWLEDGEMENT

I would like to appreciate my beautiful daughter Anuoluwapo for giving me the motivation to write this book because I know that one day, it will serve as her guide. My gratitude is to my lovely wife, Victoria for providing immense support and encouragement from the inception of the book to the closing. To my wonderful parents, Elder and Deaconess Niyi Ogunjinmi who have been married for more than 44 years, you lay a great foundation and exemplify a true marriage.

To my second parents, Pastor and Mrs. Olaolu Makinde, thank you for your constant love and support. Also, I thank my brother Tunde for always being there to support and inspire great conversations. I want to say a big thank you to everyone who saw me through the journey of the book and contributed one way or another to its success. Above all, I'm grateful to God who made this experience fulfilling and fun. He is the original Author of the book and I'm just a mouthpiece.

I dedicate this book to all who struggle to find true love and experience "happily-ever after."

FOREWORD

Men are dogs who only want one thing!

Understanding men is impossible!

All the good ones are taken!

I have been coaching women to become man whisperers for years and find that *Revelations of Relationship* is a valuable resource for women searching for genuine love. If you are stuck on the crazy cycle of relational demise and you're at a loss for what to do, then this how-to guide is for you. Femi provides biblical principles and practical tools to eradicate the I-can't-find-a-good-man excuses. With concise nuggets of wisdom and honest assessments gleaned from years of experience and divine inspiration, he empowers you to transition from doormat to dominate.

I met Femi several years ago while promoting my novel, *The Forbidden Secrets of the Goody Box*. As a guest on his show, we discussed the perils of dating and how to avoid them. His insight about dating from a Christian man's perspective exposed women to the mystical man code.

Women with "man" problems tend to seek advice from other women: mother, sisters and girlfriends. Although they may have your best interest at heart, the advice is often tainted with emotions, past experiences and a general misunderstanding of why men do what they do in relationships. Femi uses his platform to encourage women to fulfill a lifelong dream: attract, attain and marry "the one." Few have the integrity to do what Femi does without effort or selfish motives.

So if you've been nursing a broken heart, trying to re-sell single-use bridesmaid gowns or settling for less than you deserve; you'll find answers to your questions in this book!

Valerie J. Lewis Coleman, best-selling author of *The Forbidden Secrets of the Goody Box*–*Relationship advice that your father didn't tell you and your mother didn't know*

TheGoodyBoxBook.com

FOREWORD

The institution of marriage is as old as life itself, from the inception of creation. It is not possible to separate life or creation from marriage. To do so is to negate the purpose of God for man. This is because there can be neither fruitfulness nor multiplication without that God-ordained union called marriage.

In this book, "Revelations of Relationship", Gfem has craftily identified the keys to a good beginning of a lasting marriage, and a directional insight to its divine destination. It is one thing to be in marriage, and yet another thing to navigate through it successfully. This book will help the reader to understand that the longest – staying marriage is not necessarily the most successful, especially if the partners are merely but enduring each other. Hence, I give 'thumbs up' to Gfem for delving into the very foundations of bliss as touching a sustainable and successful marital relationship.

By the grace of God, marriage counseling is one of the thriving arms of my Ministry, and I have perused through several books on marriage. After reading through this book by Gfem, I am compelled to say that this is indeed, a great addition to the family. I am obliged to welcome Gfem with open arms. Hence, I strongly recommend this book to everything that has breath – man or woman, young or old.

Pastor Bayo Adeyokunnu

Regional Pastor

RCCG NRA1, North America Region 1

Author: *Marriage In Spirit and Truth*;

and other Christian books

INTRODUCTION

Revelations of Relationship will revolutionize any relationship for good. People, who are lost in the world of relationships and neurotic if they will ever find a soul mate and get married, will find this book a solution to their worries. The book provides proven tips to secure and build a connection with a date. It shares secrets to a lasting relationship, and principles to stop cheating.

The inspiration came naturally through the divine help of God, coupled with my insatiable passion for helping people discover an ideal partner and maintain a healthy relationship. The book gleans from my experiences as a relationship coach influencing relationship decisions for over a decade and having helped many thousands of people find relational fulfillment.

In 2012, I began to write weekly messages on relationships and post them on social media. These write-ups were not premeditated, but divine. I received them through the Holy Spirit at odd times of the day. Either when driving to work or about to go to sleep. In the middle of the year, the Lord told me to keep what I wrote and by the end of the year, there would be a need for them. By the end of the year, the Lord dropped the idea of writing a book and incorporating my write-ups.

Revelations of Relationship not only explains some of the challenges of relationships involving finding a soul mate, dating, and sustaining marriage. It offers timeless solutions to these issues. The solutions bridge the gap between secular-relationship approaches and biblical principles.

COMMUNICATION:
THE PRESENT CONDITION(S) MAY NOT MAKE HIM A WRONG PARTNER

Your partner could be the chosen one from God and you still feel he is not right for you. A man of God could have told you he is your soul mate, but you are not convinced because your relationship is entangled with conflicts. You argue with each other over basic things and wonder, this can't be my prince charming, my helpmate. It's impossible. Many problems between partners can be attributed to ineffective communication such as lack of attention to unspoken language (body language, personal space, etc), active listening, and response instead of reaction.

Couples complain that their partners don't pay attention to them when they are being approached. Well, maybe they are approaching them at the wrong time. Someone who comes home looking frustrated or tired from work does not have time for a long conversation, get asked to do something, or get blamed for anything. At that moment, he prefers to be approached in a gentle manner, catered to, and engaged in less discussion.

As a couple, your partner does not have to tell you he's mad before you know it. One of the best ways to know someone's mood is to look at his face. Does he have a happy face or sad face? Does he look tired and less engaging when you talk to him? Is he playful when he comes home? Plan to have him relaxed if your answers are no. Take off his jacket and shoes, soak his feet in warm water, and prepare a good meal. After all these, he will be physically, mentally, and socially fit to hear all you have to say and possibly do what you want.

My dog came into my studio room one day, looked at me, and walked away. He realized by the look on my face that I was busy and didn't have time to play. As a child, if my mom looked at me in a way I knew what she meant. Nowadays, kids don't even understand their parents' body language until they are spoken to. Some of them who understand, act insubordinate, like the story of a little girl who visited her grandmother. She wanted to say something to her grandma and her mom stepped on her foot not to say it. The little girl busted out, "Mom, stop stepping on me, I want to talk." lol. This little girl understood her mom but she chose not to cooperate.

As parents, we must teach our children unspoken language because sometimes we have no strength to talk and when we talk something bad can come out of our mouths. Teach your children to read meanings to your body language. The same thing goes for couples. Paying close attention to facial expressions and moods will enhance communication and prevent arguments.

Active listening is listening objectively. It requires you to understand the other person's point of view, what he wants to communicate rather than what you want to hear. An active listener engages with the speaker, asks questions, and responds respectfully. Often times, we are after what we want to hear and usually miss the important point. If you are not an active listener then you are a passive listener. Passive listening is hearing the words, sound vibrations, and not processing them or interpreting them for the meaning intended by the speaker. A passive listener conveys no expressions or responds to the message by the speaker. He is more like a recorder.

A passive listener reacts to argument instead of responds. In the state of reactions, emotions get the best of us. They take a central role and we are not in control of the situation. That's why we get wrong results. An argument can be as small as putting down the toilet seat after being used or always turning off the bedroom light when no one is in the room. Reaction to this statement can be, "Why don't you turn it off yourself, why are you always complaining?" Reacting in this manner can exacerbate the situation.

The other side of the coin, respond, usually lives in the presence of reasoning, logic, and thought. To respond instead of react requires patience and self-control. You are driven by solution rather than trying to argue. A good response can change the direction of the conversation and quench the fire ignited by your partner. The Bible says a gentle response turns away wrath but grievous words stir up anger. In the examples stated above, a good response can be just saying, "I'm sorry, I will work on remembering next time not to do it again."

To listen actively in order to respond rather than react requires for you to put your emotions aside. How you do that is to think positively about the discourse. Find benefits in what your partner is saying. She will not just ask you to turn off the light without a concrete purpose. One of the benefits of turning off the light is to save electric bills. If you find it hard to think immediately because of how harsh you are processing the statement, count to twenty seconds to calm down. When resorted to this, your conversation is bound to be smooth, argument is prevented, and she feels she is your soul mate.

TRANSFORMATIONAL APPROACH TO DATING

One of the problems in finding a soul mate is women being the chaser. That makes women victims of their needs. Biologically, women are the receivers by the shape of their vulvas while men are givers by their own shapes. This suggests men are designed to take the initiative in asking women out. I have not read in the bible that a woman should chase a man. However, I have read that a man who finds (locates by searching) a good wife obtains favor from the Lord. Biblically, it's the will of the Lord for a man to find his woman, which comes with blessings. Socially, people are pressured and taught wrongly. So people get it wrong in their relationships. Women, embrace your femininity and work on attracting a godly man by your godliness.

How do you attract an ideal man?

After many break ups and falling into wrong relationships, single people ask rhetorical questions such as, where is the right partner? Does he exist? Yes, the right partner exists but you have been attracting the wrong one. Attraction is usually the prelude of a relationship. Our lives are basically built on attraction. What we buy is due to our attraction toward those materials. For example, you go to fashion stores to buy clothes that catch your attention. If you are not attracted to the clothes, you won't buy them. It is the same for relationships. We get involved with someone we are attracted to.

There are three principles behind attracting the right partner and these principles can be found in the word, "WHO."

W: "Where" do you hang out? Your hangout spot (s) determines the type of people you meet. If you hang out at the club, you probably meet party-oriented people. If you hang out at business seminar, a high chance exists you will run into business-savvy people and entrepreneurs. Hanging out at the right place increases your chances of meeting the person you desire.

Start by describing the person you want to marry. List his profile, attributes, and then think about exact locations and events where this kind of person would most likely hang out. For example, if you are seeking a Christian man, and one of his attributes is to love serving God, a best location to find that individual is the church. He could be playing an instrument, singing, volunteering in one of the departments (Ushering, Security, Protocol, Technical, Drama, etc) or serving as one of the coordinators for church events.

H: "How" do you dress? When we look at our culture today, we see men in sagging pants, feeling it's a cool fashion but it's not. The history of sagging pants began in the prison system, as many sources point out. In prison, belts are not allowed to be worn because they can be used as weapon or as a means to suicide. It's also a symbol an inmate uses to convey to another that he's sexually available or just recently taken. A polished, educated, and respectable lady will not be attracted to a man whose pant sags.

Likewise, women, when you walk around with clothes that reveal your body and upload them on social media, the men who are attracted to you are those who go after what they see. The only intent the men will have is to make you a conquest. When you see the person you want to attract, it's important that you look the part because you are addressed by how you dress. If you don't want to be called a wrong name, be looked down upon, and miss out on the opportunity of meeting your future partner, then look decent and presentable.

O: "Out" of all your friends, which one has the right character and positive influence? If you have none, then you need to leave that group of friends. There is a popular saying that birds of the same feather flock together. When you hang out with the wrong crowd, it's challenging for a potential soul mate to discern the good from the bad.

People are very particular about who they date, because they don't want to be involved with people who have a history of sleeping around and unpleasant attitudes. So they put on their detective hats and find out the kind of person you are. They gather information about you and the crew you roll with. If a man for example finds out a couple of your girl friends have bad reputations, he makes the decision right there of not pursuing you.

It may not be the ideal way of finding out if the girl is a marriage material because the girl could actually be a good girl and just happened that her friends' reputations are not impressive and nothing to write home about. Nonetheless, it is a method that people often resort to and most times, they work. Your character and morals are very precious to men and take precedence over artificial objects.

I understand you want to look beautiful as a lady. While you are enhancing your outer beauty with Mary Kay, Mac, and other beauty products, do the same with your inner beauty. A saying in Yoruba language by the Yoruba tribe in Nigeria is: "Iwa lewa," meaning your character is your beauty. When a man introduces you to his family, your character is always a strong fundamental they examine.

In order for you to attract an ideal partner, hang out at the right place, dress appropriately, and surround yourself with the right people. You are a prey (Treasure Jewel) to the hunter (Men). As a prey you have to be a mouthful to last the hunter till eternity so that you satiate the hunter. Ensure you are beautiful in and out because when a hunter sees an attractive prey, he goes for it.

HOW TO STOP CHEATING

I have often heard women say they will be okay if their man cheats on them with an upgrade (i.e., someone with better looks, job, status, achievement, etc.) than a downgrade. So I asked these women their rationale. They felt that it's disrespectful for their men to cheat with a downgrade. But doesn't it show that their men can do better than them if they cheat with an upgrade? Does that make them respect their men more because they can do better than them? Or does it make them feel that the man must have loved them enough for them to still remain in the relationship and not leave them for an upgrade? No matter how you look at the situation, it does not change the fact that he cheated. Don't make yourself feel good or better if it's an upgrade.

First things first, find out why he cheated. A man who cheats with either an upgrade or downgrade shows that he found something in that woman that may be missing in you. Other times, the man is just promiscuous. As one of my radio talk-show guests expressed in an interview, "A man cheats on his wife because the side chick is UGLY." In this context, UGLY does not necessary mean a physical description but a character description of a woman. UGLY is an acronym for Understanding, Gratifying, Loving, and Yielding women. Men enjoy a woman who understands, a woman who won't complain too much, and will cherish the time you spend with her.

A gratifying woman is a woman who praises her man both at home and outside. She makes statement like, "You are the best thing that has ever happened to me. I love you so much, you can have it anywhere, anytime." Those statements stroke a man's ego. A gratifying woman feels one of her goals is to please her husband as she embraces the scripture, I Corinthians 7:4 "The wife gives authority over her body to her husband, and the husband also gives authority over his body to his wife." Therefore they don't deprive each other of sexual relations. Men appreciate a yielding woman who is willing to comply with what he says, basically being submissive.

The point of view by no means defends that a good reason exists for anybody to cheat on each other, but for women to realize what they might be doing wrong, which leads their partners outside. No one should cheat on each other. If there seems to be any reason to cheat, then the issue should be discussed among the partners and rectified. My wife and I both believe that we are God's chosen partners for each other, therefore there shouldn't be anybody better qualified for each other in all areas to fulfill whatever we might be looking for from another person. For God to choose us as the bone and flesh of each other means no better match exists.

Cheating is a form of abuse as it affects the emotions of the victim. There are many levels of consequences for cheating. It destroys lives, relationship, truncates destinies, and easily tears families apart. Athletes such as Shaquille O'Neal, Tiger Woods, and so many others lost their marriages and money as a result of cheating. When parents divorce as a result of infidelity, it affects the future of the children. Divorcing is telling your children it's okay for them to grow up and divorce. The seed of divorce continues to grow and repeat itself from one generation to another.

My mom always told me that marrying someone from a broken family is not palatable and I stuck to it. Imagine having many men out there with a mom like mine, the chance of us marrying a woman from a broken family is slim to none. By the way, some states (Illinois, South Dakota, Hawaii, North Carolina, Mississippi, New Mexico, and Utah) have a legal recourse for married people called Alienation of Affection. The lawsuit is brought by a deserted spouse against a third-party alleged to be responsible for the failure of the marriage. This act should be able to deter outside influences on marriages, but it is not adopted by all the states.

Paul and Janet had been dating since college and after graduation got engaged. They were living in two different cities during their engagement period when Paul cheated and got another girl, Precious, pregnant. Janet was not aware that Paul had cheated. Paul told Precious to abort the baby because he was about to get married and did not want to be with her. Precious, enraged, decided if she could not have him, then nobody else would. Precious picked up her car, drove to Janet's apartment and shot her dead. Janet was unaware her man was cheating and died painfully for a sin she did not commit. For minutes of pleasure, Paul risked his relationship, and his fiancé's life.

Men have asked me if it is possible to stop cheating. Anything is possible in life as long as you apply yourself. Nothing happens without being first conceived in the mind. People go after what they have purposed in their hearts. When men say they don't know how it happened and they will stop is an excuse. Women know you won't stop but they give you the benefit of doubt to prove yourself. Perhaps a few of those men desire to stop but they don't know how to prevent themselves from looking outside. Women are not exceptions to cheating either because they do. Most times, women cheat because of an issue in the relationship, and men cheat because there is an opportunity.

In order to stop cheating:

You must first purpose in your heart that you are ready to give it up. One must come to terms with himself that it is time to put the cheating life style away. Once that is established, find a genuine strong rationale why you want to stop. That rationale will be a motivation and a picture that will come to mind and prevent you when chanced to cheat again.

If your reason is not strongly cemented in your mind, it is possible for you to forget and easily be persuaded to cheat, especially when among people who are promiscuous. I watched the life of a man who used to be heavily involved with drugs and later stopped because he didn't want to miss out on his daughter's life and be visited in jail. Anytime he thinks about drugs, his daughter comes to mind. His daughter is his strong rationale and motivation that restricts him.

(2a) There has to be a genuine repentance of your sin. Your body has been polluted and the blood of Jesus needs to cleanse you and make you new again. When you cheat, a part of the person you cheated with is left with you, and her spirit has influence on you. There has to be God's intervention to purge all the unwanted spirits in your body.

Cheaters usually have stories of sleeping with other people in their dreams. One reason is that the spirits of the people they slept with are battling with them. Second reason is the spirit of incubus and succubus. Incubus is a male demon having sexual intercourse with women in their sleep. Succubus is a female demon having sexual intercourse with men in their sleep.

When you repent, all these unwanted spirits will be gone and God will forgive you all your sins. 1 John 1:9 says, "If we confess our sins, He is faithful and just to forgive us our sins and to cleanse us from all unrighteousness." Say these short prayers to repent: "Father, I'm a sinner and I have fallen short of your glory. I've come to terms with myself and never to visit my iniquities again. Please forgive me and I receive you as my Lord and my Savior."

(b) Call the Holy Spirit to intervene. In addition to your prayers for repentance, ask God to send the Holy Spirit. The Holy Spirit gives you conscience; it turns your mind away from committing fornication, adultery, and fills your mind with positive thoughts. The spirit speaks the truth and reminds you of your rationale whenever the flesh is willing. Having the Holy Spirit will guide you against going back to old ways.

(3) This deals with the crowd you hang out with, the activities and events that you attend. Exposure to sexual-oriented activities such as nightclubs, strip clubs, and promiscuous friends need to be avoided. Otherwise, your mind and body will be tempted and easily be overcome. If indeed you have become born again and changed, then old things have to pass away and never be revisited. When surrounded with friends who always cheat on their partners, their acts will influence you to do the same. If going to clubs and seeing a lot of women in kinky outfits turn you on and makes you think about cheating, then you need to refrain from that social scene and attend church social events or other positive events with like-minded people.

A young man decided to stop going to clubs after giving his life to Jesus. One day, his friends convinced him to follow them to the club. He decided not to go inside and wait for his friends outside. He did not know when he started tapping his feet to the sound of the music coming from the club. Before he realized it, he was back inside to his old lifestyle. You need to be around the right kind of crowd and attend events that will not expose you to that old lifestyle.

Don't let the fidelity contract of your relationship expire or get terminated. Fidelity is like an egg. Once broken, it's difficult to put back together. Be mature, responsible, and respectful of your partner and relationship. Don't let the blood of someone else come from your hand. Though Paul did not kill his fiancée directly, however, indirectly he murdered her. For the love of your partner and sake of humanity, quit infidelity.

LOVE MAKES YOU BLIND, MARRIAGE RESTORES YOUR SIGHT

Partners hide from one another some aspects of their lives such as events and unpleasant characters before they get marry. After the big wedding day, true character begins to show. But disclosing aspects of your life that you deem important prior to vows will save the marriage from crumbling and prevent you from looking at your partner as untrustworthy. Once trust is betrayed, it takes a long time to regain. Sometimes that trust may not be regained, leading to a break up. A best practice is for couple to get to know each other, spend substantial amount of time understanding and revealing things to one another before getting married.

Now, just because you spent five years dating before getting married does not mean you fully know your partner. Both of you are still spending each day discovering and knowing some part about the other person. So you may not fully know your partner in X amount of years. That time though helps you to uncover some characteristics, lifestyle, and family issues that are necessary to know before marriage, and need to be addressed in order for that marriage to be planted on a fertile and healthy ground. Some of these things you will discover about your partner before marriage can be heartbreaking and can prevent the relationship from progressing. Perhaps it is better to know them now rather than later. Hopefully, you can live with some of those things.

A broken courtship or engagement is better than a broken marriage. I know a couple that did not make it to the altar because the girl lied about her job position, graduating from undergrad, and couple of other lies. It was not because of these lies that the guy broke the relationship. It was because the girl kept these secrets from him for so long. If those secrets were revealed at an early stage, the guy could have forgiven her and still remained in the relationship.

When your partner reveals his current or past dreadful stories, it is not the time to be judgmental. One of the reasons people hold back from divulging their secrets is because they feel their partners will judge them and possibly opt out of the relationships. But sometimes those pasts happened when the person was still naïve, being youthful, or circumstances beyond her control. Therefore she can be forgiven. No one is beyond mistakes and we all have pasts.

What is important is to know the truth about your partner rather than someone outside telling you. That's what relationship is about; being fully aware of your partner's past, present, and plans for the future. Nobody should know your partner better than you except his siblings or parents with whom he has spent most of his life. You are the new sheriff in town now, so you should know enough about your partner.

CONNECTION:
AN IMPORTANT ASPECT OF DATING

Technology now limits true connection, which is an important aspect of relationships. Just because you meet someone on cyber space, have a great chemistry online, talking over the phone, and text messages does not mean you will have great chemistry when you meet in person. All that poking, winks on social media do not truly express how deeply an interest the person has and if he is right fit for you. The profile picture can be deceiving and fake. It can be an old picture that does not represent what the person looks like presently. There has to be a face-to-face meeting to have a true connection.

People choose different locations for first dates based on their reasons. I will shy away from scheduling happy hour as a first date just because it usually takes place at a lounge. Being in a lounge environment encourages you to drink alcohol. Drinking impairs the quality of conversation and can affect people differently. You might be sure how it affects you and very unsure how it affects the other person.

You may end up drinking excessively inadvertently and therefore lose control.

This can cause you to ask the guy to follow you home or drop you at home. At that point this is not a casual date. It has undermined the essence of the first date. The guy is not supposed to know your house on the first date or you know his. He should not land on your couch or your bed. That will make the guy consider you as being cheap and think you do the same to every guy you meet on the first date. I would also avoid going to the movies because it takes away from the actual focus of the date and cuts into your conversation.

Where should you choose for your first date?

A woman needs to have a casual face-to-face meeting at a location of her choice. Places where you are comfortable to talk and where people are around. This practical step secures your safety to an extent. Safety is always important to consider when meeting people, especially the first time. The first date is about chatting about each other's likes, activities that you enjoy doing, the type and nature of your job, school you went to, a little bit about your background, and what each person does after work and on weekends.

You can accomplish these in a lunch date, which will not take more than an hour. There is nothing to lose. The location can be at a caribous, where you can talk over a coffee. If it's summer time, you can also take a walk or have a sit-down conversation at a park. This will allow you to understand the person, his personality, if he can carry a conversation, if any chemistry exists, and similar activities you find in common that can excite a second date.

As a man, if the girl asked you to schedule a first date, avoid scheduling one to an expensive restaurant because some women go out with multiple men a week with no or little purpose of dating them but just using them for lunch or dinner. Avoid being used for a meal. Don't take a woman to an expensive restaurant on a first date, especially if you cannot keep up with it when you are finally in relationship with her. I understand you want to go all out to impress her on the first date, but she can assume that's a lifestyle you can afford.

Women easily get comfortable with nice and beautiful treatment. Whatever hand you use to pick up a lady that is the hand she will get familiar with. If you cannot keep up with it, don't give a taste of it and have her thirst for more. Women will not agree to start with a high-end five-star restaurant and then downsize later to a two-star restaurant. Women love upgrades not downgrades of lifestyle. It makes more sense to be conservative and then step it up a notch when you can afford a better lifestyle. Caribou and taking a walk are inexpensive first dates.

CONFUSION OF WOMEN
WHEN DATING

Women often believe when they connect intellectually, emotionally, and intimately with a man that means the man is in love. Also, if the man brings her home to his siblings, that automatically suggests he's interested in her. Sure he's interested, but might actually be engrossed in a different thing. You probably think he's interested in taking that relationship to the next level and making you a wife. On the other hand, he's thinking about getting into your pants and deceiving you to think otherwise.

A man uses this strategy to make you think he's taking that relationship seriously by bringing you home to his parents or siblings so that you can give up the cookie. Especially for a man who lives with his parents, bringing you home means nothing. The parents probably allow him to bring as many women he chooses because he's considered an adult. Don't be deceived and get your hopes high when these things happen. You will find he's just playing you.

One of the best things to do in a confusing situation like this is to sit the guy down and have a mature conversation with him of where the relationship is going and make sure you are reading between the lines of his words. No need exists to be confused about your status in a relationship and how the relationship is shaping. You have invested your emotions, time, and loyalty in the relationship. Therefore, you are entitled to know exactly what's going on, if the partnership has a future. No one needs to be misled.

When you sit him down, tell him in a gentle non-emotional voice that you are in the relationship because you love him and if he's no longer interested, or does not see the relationship the way you see it, that is fine. Express that you are not desperate and not trying to force him to do anything or commit to what he does not want. You just want to know where you guys stand and if that suggests any future together or this is where the relationship ends.

Speaking from a logical and non-emotional state makes the guy comfortable to talk and realize indeed this girl loves him and at the same time isn't going to chop his head off if he's no longer interested. Some men hold back telling the woman they are no longer interested or don't see themselves getting married to her because they are afraid of hurting the woman, knowing how much feeling and time she has invested. When the man does not see a comfortable avenue of coming clean, he will drag out the relationship until the woman gets it that he's no longer interested. At that point the woman will be the one to break up instead of him.

Men in this situation want to avoid being blamed that they broke up the relationship. It is important for the woman to put aside emotions and anger in her voice in order to get the authentic word from her man. Otherwise, he will lie to your face and tell you what you want to hear and not what you need to know.

PERSISTENT CHARACTER

Some people are single today because they have changed their true characters from good to bad due to ill ordeals with wrong partners. Just because their partners cheated on them, jilted them, left them at the altars, broke off the engagements, they have determined to put up a wall and/or treat the opposite sex wrongly. I truly understand your pain. However, the truth is you are only hurting yourself more. You are blowing your chance of attracting the right partner. No one wants to stand a partner with bad character. When you stay true to your good moral and character, you have a high chance of meeting an ideal partner who will treat you right.

Staying true to your good character requires that you are completely healed from your past relationships before going to another one. Women, being emotional people, do not like being alone. This pushes them to quickly jump from one man to the next. It is not a nice way to start a good relationship. When you are not totally healed from an old relationship, the new guy picks from your baggage and men don't like that. When you have not gotten over your ex, you are bitter, and have occasional moodiness. It is impossible to totally be yourself one hundred percent when you are still holding on to a past.

Things of the past will influence and conflict with the current relationship. The new guy will have hard time figuring you out. You will appear as bipolar when he sees the good side of you today and the bad side tomorrow. It slows the progress of the relationship because no guy wants to be with someone he does not fully know. A guy who is not patient and not comfortable with you will opt out of that relationship. Maybe at the time of his decision you are beginning to fall for him, then his decision comes and that will put you back to where you were before you met him, which is single and depressed.

It is very important to take time to heal before jumping into a new relationship. It's like an athlete who is supposed to take six months off from a leg injury but went back to playing within a month. He will get injured again and go right back on the bench because he was not fully healed before he went back to playing. Constantly work on your character. A bad character is like a flat tire; it will get you nowhere. Doing all these will guarantee a healthy relationship.

How do you become healed from old Relationships?

(1) Have closure with the person who offended you. Talk to him about how disappointed you are and how deeply you were hurt by what he did. Most importantly, ask him why he did what he did. Getting to the bottom of the matter,

gives better light to the issue. The book of Proverbs: 4:7 says, "Wisdom is the principal thing; therefore get wisdom: and with all thy getting get understanding." When you understand why people do what they do, it's the most crucial step to resolve the matter.

A man used to smack his five-year-old daughter for sucking her thumb. He smacked her several times, with no sign of her stopping. Later he had an epiphany to ask the daughter why she sucks her thumb. The answer was shocking to him. The little girl said because "I'm bored." The father felt pity for smacking her all this while. He told her anytime she was bored, she should find something else to do. He was able tell her different things she could do when bored instead of sucking her thumb. You will be amazed that the resolution to solving the matter and letting go of the hurt resides in the rationale.

(2) Learn to forgive the perpetrator. Even if you don't have closure, forgiveness alone is enough. Matthew 6:15 say, "But if you do not forgive others their sins, your Father will not forgive your sins." I'm sure we offend God so many times, going against His will, and we want Him to forgive us. When you are harboring a matter and somebody inside your heart, you are basically in your own prison. You are not free. The person has control over your emotions, dictates how you think and act. It is better to free the person, and their bad energy.

Just say, "Father, I want to forgive this man, he has hurt me, and I release him to you now. Take control." If you say that, you will feel a heavy burden lifted from you. What is ahead is way better than what you have gone through. Don't let the person and the matter stand as a stumbling block of your happiness and moving forward.

Let go of your past and turn over a new chapter today to stay faithful to your good character and morals. That way, the one God has chosen for you will draw near to stay. It is not good to pay back evil with evil. Just because you were jilted does not mean everybody you meet is going to do the same. Be open-minded and give chances. Life is about taking chances but well-calculated ones.

KEYS TO RELATIONSHIP SUSTAINABILITY

Until you discover something more than sex in a woman and more than finances in a man, you may never truly appreciate your partner. One of the two biggest demands (money and sex) in relationships may not be present all the time. When they are absent, should you leave or look for someone else who can fill the void? There is something more substantial and fundamental to sustain relationships and that is: Love and Respect. In addition are Leadership, Fulfilling your end of the deal, and Building positive memories.

Many needs and wants exist in marriage by man and woman. However, primary needs exist that most men and women will both agree to. Respect is one of the keys to sustaining relationships for men, while love is for women. Ephesians 5: 33 says: "Nevertheless, each one of you (Men) must also love his own wife as he loves himself, and the wife must respect her husband." Respect and love are expensive needs in the relationship. Respect is dear to men and love is dear to women.

I had a discussion with a guest on my radio talk show about the issue of women respecting their husbands. My guest said there is nowhere in the bible that says husbands must earn respect. Rather, he earns his respect by virtue of his position. This challenges the society's view that you earn respect based on merit, what you do. If a woman can respect, which also means submit to her husband irrespective of the differences in financial status, academics, or career level, she's bound to enjoy her husband and marriage. In all, submit to one another out of reverence to God.

Love has been a great debate and controversial topic in society. Many have their own take on love but I will draw my own reference from 1 Corinthians 13:4-7, "Love is patient, love is kind. It does not envy, it does not boast, it is not proud. It does not dishonor others, it is not self-seeking, it is not easily angered, it keeps no record of wrongs. Love does not delight in evil but rejoices with the truth. It always protects, always trusts, always hopes, always perseveres."

If you are not fulfilling the aforementioned as a husband, then you do not love your wife. If you are not yet married and cannot exhibit the characteristics of love, then you are not ready to be a husband. I will recommend you print out this part of the scripture and put in a place you can see every day to remind you of what love is. These are the requirements that satisfy that a man loves his wife.

Every man is created with a leadership trait and as a man you want to lead by example. You want to be able to lead a relationship whereby your wife trusts you, believes in you, and has confidence in your directions. The Bible says in Genesis 18:19: "For I know him, that he will command his children and his household after him, and they shall keep the way of the LORD, to do justice and judgment; that the LORD may bring upon Abraham that which he hath spoken of him."

Women look forward to this type of man with leadership traits, one who is ready to walk the family in the right path. A man who is ready to lead his family must be able to seek God's face, hear what God has for him. Otherwise he will be leading with his own knowledge and that will fail him. A man is like a blind man; he needs somebody with foresight or a cane to tell him what is ahead. Without the man with foresight or a cane, the blind man will fall all the time. God serves as the man with the foresight and a cane for us because He sees what is ahead.

Consistency in holding on to your own bargain in the deal is another essential key to relationship sustainability. There is this saying that, "Don't marry someone who you can live with, marry someone you cannot live without." Marrying someone you cannot live without means doing what it takes to keep your partner. It shows that you value the person so much and don't want to risk losing him.

When a relationship falls apart, in essence, one or both parties have failed to do what it entails to keep each other. Relationship is not about being selfish or self centered. It is about the commitment to give up ego, and sacrifice personal time and resources to please each other. Relationship is hundred/hundred, not fifty/fifty. You give all you've got! You are in it to satisfy each other's urges, wants, and needs.

If you are still thinking that you have to please yourself first then you got it wrong. Pleasing yourself first only happens when you are single, when you only worry about yourself. Once you get married, that option no longer exists. Don't take each other for granted. Focus on meeting each other's desires and that will sustain your relationship.

Positive memory is also a great influence to sustaining relationships. When you build good memories, your relationship is strengthened. People break up and make up because they remember the good old times. Clients come back to you for your service(s) because they were pleased with your work and hence, they remember you. The positive memories still linger in their minds and draw them back. Some people left their jobs and were hired back because the companies have their track records of accomplishments. Leaving a bad taste in people's mouths undermines your relationship with them.

The ways you can build good memories is to take vacations occasionally with your partner. It doesn't have to be a long one. It can be a weekend vacation at a nearby city or a beautiful hotel in your city. Do occasional dates as well. Take her to restaurant. Money doesn't have to be an excuse, for example you can cook if you are not the one that regularly cooks in the family. That is romantic for ladies. Most romantic activities don't cost too much and for women, it is the thought that counts.

A woman expressed to me that her husband stopped loving her the way she wanted. I asked her, what way? She replied, "He stopped doing those things he did to get me."

Without her giving all the details, I knew what she meant. What keeps the fire of love burning is to keep dating, and performing those things you did when you were trying to woo her. You know those beautiful things you did. It could be random love text messages, poems you read, love letters, or good surprises. When you are no longer in the picture, you want people to remember you for good deeds. Begin to plant those good seeds and build that lasting memory.

FRIEND ZONE

Men don't know how to avoid being on women's "Nice-guy list." If you don't know what a nice-guy list is, it is a list of guys that women enjoy their company as friends but it only goes as far as that. Women don't see themselves dating or being together with the nice guy in the future. They don't see themselves being intimate, holding hands, kissing, etc. There is absence of feelings from the woman's perspectives. You are technically a guy friend but the lady relates to you as one of her home girls. I'm not saying being friends is bad but be careful how far you take that friendship if you are actually interested in the girl.

Here are some signs that you are in the friend zone: (1) If you are spending long hours on the phone with the girl and what she's talking to you about is how she's in love with some other guy, how they went out and had fun. (2) If she is persistently seeking your advice on how to get with another guy (3) If she is seeking your advice on how to make her current relationship better (4) You are the one she calls when the boyfriend breaks her heart all the time. If she's looking for a shoulder to cry on, empathy, then she sees you as another female friend and you are in the friend zone.

Another type of friendship like this is a friend with benefits, which involves sex. But being in a friend zone exists without sex or any form of intimacy. Nice guys think women owe them something, as if they are obligated to be in a relationship with them. Let me tell you, you could have bought her ticket to movies, gave her tissues when she was crying over a break-up, paid her rent, car note, put gas in her car, bought her gift cards, shoes, attended her family functions, and still all you have done won't make the girl change how she sees you as just a friend.

In order to get out of friend zone and have the girl start to see you as a future partner, first convey your interest to the girl that you like her and would be delighted if she could consider dating, assuming you have not shared your interest with her before. Realistically, it's difficult to have a girl change how she sees you and then decide to date you. Only a few cases have turned out like this and yours is about to be added to the list. If she says no a few times, don't beg her and stop talking.

Second is to let your actions speak now because women get it more with the actions. Reduce picking up her calls all the time. When you do talk to her and she's talking about some other guys, cut the conversation short and give her an excuse that you have something else to do. The next thing is to find you another attractive female friend with whom you spend time and hang out once in a while. Make sure you are not leading the new girl on because you are really not interested in being with her; you are just interested in casual friendship. So don't be that guy who will do what is wrong.

When you hang out with this new girl, make sure you guys attend events the other girl will be attending. Women get jealous when they see another girl with a guy who is interested in them. Now the old girl thinks the reason you don't spend so much time with her on the phone anymore is the new girl. She feels the new girl is the one taking your time and you are no longer available to her as you used to be. Women don't like another woman taking all the perks they get from a guy. The old girl will begin to see the other side you want her to see, which she was not seeing before. Give it few weeks. The old girl will come back, making moves to be with you.

THE COMPLEMENT

Men complain that women don't want to date them. They are being turned down and sometimes avoided when they want to spark a conversation. Here is a secret about women that men may not know and either women are conscious about it or not. Women are actively seeking a man to complement them. Women prefer to be with a man who completes and makes them whole at all levels (physical, spiritual, moral, etc.).

The physical aspect entails education, finances, fashion, network, looks, height, etc. The spiritual aspect involves being equally yoked, serving the same God, knowledgeable about the Bible, someone who attends church and is involved in church activities or is a worker rather than a member. The moral level is tied to the guy's values and traditions. Our backgrounds and cultures shape our thinking and influence our belief systems.

What we consider good or bad, right or wrong can be a result of our traditions and culture. If you come from a culture that sees one thing in a particular way, your partner can see it the other way around if she's from another culture. For example, in Nigerian culture, kids can live with their parents till they get married with full support from their parents. The legal adult age in American culture is (18) eighteen, which means the parents can have the children out of the house at that age to be on their own, be independent, and get married.

Sadly, the physical level carries more weight. Women don't want a downgrade. They prefer a man above them even though we see cases of women settling with a man on the same level or below. On the other side, men can overlook some areas about women when they are making their selections because men are viewed as breadwinners and there are more expectations for us than women. Men can decide the educational background of women does not matter. Just like back in the days African men would travel to their villages to go marry a young girl with no educational background. It still happens today.

Men should not expect women who dress well to be attracted to them when they are not on point with their style of look. I see single women at church functions with attractive styles of dressing but the men barely look the part. Men out there still wear baggy clothes, loose shirts, and saggy pants. All that fashion style does not cut it. Start wearing fitted clothes and suits. If you have to lose weight, then do so. Exercising will help your health and prevent unwanted disease. Deodorant and fragrance should also be your best friend.

I met a guy some years back in college, Morgan State University. The school has a bridge where students hang out. Especially during summertime, you find a lot of guys there checking out the ladies walking by. This guy used different cologne when walking on the bridge to class. Upon getting to class, he switched to another cologne. You can say that is too much and has cologne fetish but truth be told, he understands and values the importance of smelling good.

In simplicity, you always attract to whom you see in the mirror. It's rare to see a fat person attracting and ending up in a relationship with a skinny person. Life is about energy and you want to be surrounded with a person who has the same or better energy than you. When you constantly work on yourself academically, spiritually, physically, financially, etc, eventually you will find the same person of equal status or better.

DIFFERENT FOLKS, DIFFERENT STROKES

The silent relationship killer to which people don't pay much attention is comparing their relationship to another. Albeit the reason behind the comparison might be positive, the outcome is negative. When we compare our relationships to a friend's relationship or to previous ones, you are actually saying you prefer to be in the shoes of your friend or go back to the old relationship. Just because your relationship is not great, juxtaposing it to another kills the relationship.

You will hear couples complain, "This guy makes tea for his wife everyday and you don't do the same for me. This woman cooks all the time for her man but you barely cook around the house. How come you don't take me out like person X takes his girl out? How come your career is not advancing like this person's? Why don't you open the car door for me as my neighbor does for his wife?" All that complaining tears your home apart little by little.

Jim and Lynda were a young college kids, dating and getting to know one another. Although physically attracted to each other, they were not compatible character-wise. They were always arguing and not on the same page. Lynda and Jim were best friends with another couple, Greg and Kim. Lynda complained to Jim about what he was not doing for her and what Greg was doing for Kim.

Greg bought Kim flowers and surprise ticket to Akon's concert. Lynda said, "Your friend bought tickets for my friend, how come you didn't buy me the same thing and you know I like Akon." Jim bought the ticket and took her to the concert but her statement was the last straw. Shortly after, Jim broke off the relationship.

Women hate to be compared to other women, but men especially hate the comparison game more. If you want your partner to change his behavior, lead by example and have your partner follow. Using an example of another man is quite demeaning to your partner. You are in a relationship to build each other up, not tear each other down.

Another thing to avoid is having a laundry list of actions you want your man to change or improve. Identify one thing and let him work on it for a while. Men cannot handle multiple things at one time because we are not wired that way. That's why you can send your man to the grocery store to buy four items, and he will end up calling you from the store, asking what you told him to buy. He might even come back home with only two things lol.

Practice one change at a time. Slow and steady wins the race. Give him time to practice and master that one change. It takes time for the change to become second nature. You might see him make the change today and tomorrow he forgets about it. Instead of getting mad, remind him. He's a work in progress. People often say men are like babies. We are, truth be told.

Another point is to avoid keeping track of how many times he does it wrong. Keep track of the times he gets it right and reward him for doing that. It can sound childish to reward a grown man for a little thing you ask him to consistently do. Remember, that little thing is important to you. Reward for a positive action is important.

The reward does not have to be monetary or buying a gift. It can be as smooth as just saying, "Babe, thank you for taking your time doing this or thank you for remembering to put the trash out or put the sponge where it belongs, or the toilet seat down..." People love to be appreciated and noticed for something good they do and once that appreciation is offered, it encourages them to reiterate that action.

By the way, the toilet seat is a common complaint in most families and the pressing of the toothpaste at the wrong spot instead from the bottom. A question that came to mind was why should men always have to put the toilet seat down for the women? When we look at it closely, women sit on the toilet seat to urinate and prefer not to take the extra effort of lifting up the seat before urinating. So they want men to already put the seat down for them. How come women don't lift up the toilet seat for men? Because when men urinate, the seat has to be up. Doesn't this whole toilet seat situation sound like double standard? It's something to think about.

FAMILY TIME

The biggest commodity in the family is not sex or money. It's time! Sex does not happen unless you have the time for it and you don't make money unless there is time committed to work for that money. You practically cannot do anything without the time dedicated for that task. I'm sure you have heard the phrase time is money. It is money because we have placed a high demand on money rather than the driver of the money itself. If money is way more important than your family, then think again. The motivation for most people to work is because they need the money to take care of their families.

Family is important and people are allowing the use of technology (phones, ipads) and work to take their time from families. We even spend more time with friends and attending all social gatherings together. It is essential to have daily quality time with your family. I'm not saying work and spending time with your friends and gadgets are not essential but what is the essence of work if you don't have the time to spend that money with whom you care and love so much? Ridiculous work hours have put a strain on family time. Some people work more than sixty hours a week because of money.

I agree there is not enough time in a day, but here is what you can do:

Whatever activities you have going on, engage your family with them. Carry them along and let them partake in them. That is still called family time. That brings the family together. For example, a man after leaving his first job in the evening picks up his family and takes them to see his drivers for the trucking side-business he has. On the way, he's conversing and interacting with his family.

Exercise the Ten-Minute Rule

When you stop other things and focus on the family, you are also spending time together. Devote at least thirty-minutes of your time daily spending time with the kid (s) and partner immediately when you get home. Do what I call the ten-minute rule of detachment and attachment. I stop thinking about work and other things ten-minutes before I get home. I basically detach my brain from those things and start connecting my brain to family.

Not to say my family is not on my mind all day but I probably didn't dedicate one-hundred-percent attention to focus on them. The ten-minute rule allows me to brainstorm what I can do with them upon getting home, what I can buy on the way home for them, and how I can make them feel good for that evening. This can work for you as

well and you can extend the ten minutes to how many minutes it can take you to brainstorm.

By the time I play with my daughter, talk to my wife
about her day and what to have for dinner, the thirty-minutes is already up. Then I can go do some personal things
for a while and then later come back to the family again
for dinner and another round of family time.

PICK-UP LINE

While among a few panelists at a conference, I was asked at the end of the relationship discussion to offer a pick up line. I said, "Sweetheart, I see this dress you are wearing on Hollywood Stars but you wear it better." After the event, I thought of another way of rephrasing it that can make it more presentable: "Sweetheart, I only see this dress you are wearing on Hollywood Stars, you must be a Star." Some women can find these lines rusty and others find them attractive. A good pick-up line can get you a girl's number and bad one can leave you embarrassed.

Men get pressured and anxious of what to tell a lady. We wrack our brains on how to approach them, the good line that will make us sound smooth and collected so they can talk to us. But we fail to realize a pick-up line is a sentence or a few sentences you say to grab the attention of a person. People are taught many lines but another man may have used those lines with the girl. Another possibility is that you try those lines with different girls and eventually you run out of lines.

Avoid using lines other people have used. Try to come up with your own unique, authentic lines that will have the girl respond to you. Women know when you are trying to play games with them and you want to avoid being put in that category. The best thing is to take the girl off guard and have her not have the initial thought that you want to talk to her. That allows her to open up to you more.

Authentic pick-up lines are dependent on the situation and environment you and the lady you are trying to talk to are in. It requires you to be spontaneous and original. Here are a few lines to exemplify my point: If you are at a bus stop trying to catch a bus and you see an attractive young lady, say, "Excuse me, Miss, it's my first time catching the bus, do you know how long the bus runs?" The lady will look at you from the position of someone who is interested in the bus and not her, thus she will provide you with a good response. That gives you a starting point and you can build the conversation from there.

Assuming you have been eyeing a young lady in your church and you are wondering how to talk to her, here is an approach: "Hello, sister, I have been seeing you in church but you have not attended our young-adult meeting, is there any reason?" Depending on the reason she gives you, follow up on it. She can say she has not had the time to attend the meeting because she has to work right after church. Then you can ask her where she works and express your hope she will be off one of these days for the meeting. Tell her when the next meeting is and say, by the way, my name is…You always want to say your name so she can remember it. My lines were different for the different scenarios that I presented.

The secret behind coming up with an original pick-up line that will grab the attention of the girl, have her listen to you, and converse, which can lead to exchange of numbers, is to look for a common factor between you and the lady. Find something that connects both of you. In my first example, it's the bus. In my second example, it's the young-adult meeting. Look for those common factors and use that to break the ice to start a conversation.

GETTING THE RING

It saddens me when I hear stories of women in relationship for so many years and there is no sign of progress. The guys have not proposed or taken them to meet their families. Perhaps they proposed long time ago and the wedding date is not yet fixed. Whenever the ladies bring up the wedding question, they try to avoid it or say it will happen soon. This is a relationship of hope with no evidence.

Ladies, how I wish you have another set of eyes to understand why your man is playing these games with you. There are men out there who are manipulators. They manipulate every situation to get what they want and after receiving what they want, they leave you to figure out they are no longer interested. There are also men who are just magicians. They are the ones that blow smoke in your face. They tell you sweet things you want to hear and make false promises.

Let me share what you don't know about men that are affecting this situation. Men want to be in a relationship with whom they love but they don't want to go extra miles to be in that relationship if there need not to. For instance, when it comes to the situation of wedding, it is discouraging for men to think of investing months and sometimes years to save thousands of dollars and blow it up one day on a ring and ceremony. That reality is hard for us to accept.

Men are thinking we can use these thousands of dollars to buy a house together, pay off some personal debts (i.e school loans), buy new cars, save for children's college, have retirement money, and go on vacation together. While you are thinking: "I have been dreaming and planning my wedding since I knew there is something called wedding. I would love to have my wonderful wedding" I get it, it's one of the special milestones you have always looked forward to. You could convince your man that the wedding means so much to you and still not cave in to your statement.

What is the real reason why he has not proposed? Give me a drum roll...........................

(1) HE IS NOT CONVINCED YOU ARE THE ONE

It's imperative to discover if he's into you and want a future together. Otherwise you are wasting your time in a relationship that could be a dead end. Sit him down and have heart to heart conversation. This is a conversation you have in a non-emotional state. Don't have the "So" called conversation. That's the angry conversation when you ask, "So where is this relationship going? So when am I going to meet your parents? So when are you going to pop the question?"

These types of questions scare a man and it's hard to get the truth out of him at that moment. He can perceive you are angry and he will abstain from saying something that may get his head cut off. In response to your questions, he will lie and tell you what you want to hear and not what you need to know! It's important to talk to him in a calm voice and a time when you feel the two of you are in a good mood i.e after a meal, during discussion about your friends or general casual non-serious topics of life.

(2) YOU HAVE ALLOWED HIM TO BECOME COMPLACENT WITH YOUR CURRENT STATUS

Men are convenient human beings. We prefer to do what is easy and comfortable; tasks and activities that don't require too much of our time and money. You could be their convenient girlfriend or fiancée that is just a string along.

How to get the ring

There are one or two action plans you can implement:

(1) Give him ultimatum. Tell him if he doesn't propose to you by a time frame, this relationship is not going to happen again. Men don't like ultimatum but if he really loves and wants to keep you, he will do it. If he still doesn't change, then you need to pull the second action plan.

(2) Break-Up to Make-Up. Men have the mentality of "If it ain't broke, don't fix it." Have you ever tried to get your man to do something around the house and he keeps procrastinating? It's because he doesn't see the urgency of fixing it. Whatever you asked him to fix still has a bit of life in it. Recently I was trying to fix a "broken" door -knob at

my house and my wife said, the door -knob has been dangling for a while. In my mind I was saying now that is broken, it needs to be fixed lol. That's just a common attitude of men; we perform damage control rather than practice prevention.

If the relationship is not broken, he's not going to fix it. Obviously your relationship still has life in it like my dangling door -knob and that's why he's not quick to action. We take you more serious when the relationship is broken. He will come back for damage control if he really loves and wants a future with you.

Maybe you are wondering if you break-up and he doesn't come back. That tells me he was never serious and in-love with you. A man that wants a future with his partner will do all it takes to salvage the relationship. Why do you want to be a string along in a relationship you don't have a plan where it's going? Don't make yourself a doormat in this relationship. You are both entitled to make plans together and agree on your journey to your marriage.

AVOIDING BASIC ARGUMENTS WITH YOUR WIFE

I have not seen any relationship where the couple doesn't experience arguments. Every relationship goes through conflicts because there are two people with different mindset, upbringing, exposure, and experience shaping their behaviors. There are however, arguments that could be avoided once we notice their frequencies.

If the arguments are not avoided, they will become a cycle and negatively impact the relationship. When we avoid arguments it will bring peace to the relationship and give the relationship oxygen to last long,

Arguments are often created by behaviors and there are typical behaviors frequently carried out by women. These are the two inevitable practices by women that piss their man off and ignite argument:

The first one has to do with the time women take to get ready for an event. Almost every man I know shares this complaint about his partner. When you are going out with your woman and she tells you she will be done in five minutes, that means you need to take off your shoes, your jacket, and take forty-five minutes nap because she's in the room trying on different clothes, shoes, putting on makeup, and getting her hair together.

This situation of course creates argument between the couple. To prevent such argument, what you do as a man is to think positively; she's dressing, making up to look good for you. Think that she's doing all that to complement you. When a woman looks good, the husband gets the credit. It's a sign that the man is taking good care of his woman.

What you can also do is proactively build her dressing time into your plan. If you want to leave the house at certain time, add extra forty-five minutes to one-hour. This will save the argument and peace will rain in your relationship.

Perhaps you feel the event you are going don't require both of you to get there at the same time and you both have personal car, I suggest to take your car and let her meet you at the event. My wife and I typically don't drive together to church because we play two different roles in church. I play drums, which requires for me to be there at certain time. So I take my personal car and she meets me in church later.

The second inevitable practice of women is talking! I read somewhere that men use an average of fifteen thousand words a day and women use twice of that. It seems to be true because women typically talk more than men. Here is a warning for men, whenever you get home in the evening and your woman still wants to talk that means she has not used all her thirty thousand words lol. So you know what you are in for. It's in the nature of women to talk, express their pain, frustration, and fills their man in on things. There is nothing wrong with that.

The problem men have is they can't bear too much talk (especially extroverted men) and they react by giving solution to what the subject of discourse is so they can end the discussion quickly. This approach does not work well with women. As a matter of fact, it adds fire to the conversation.

Women are not looking for your advice because they probably know what the solution to the problem is. What they need is a listening ear like someone to agree with them and/or empathize. And if you are quiet, it agitates them even more. It makes them feel like they are fools. There is this saying, "Silence is the best answer for a fool." I'm sure you don't want your woman to feel this way.

Here is an advice on how you handle the situation as a man

Let's say your woman is telling you how her friend Janet pissed her off earlier today. In between her narration, express few words to show that you are paying attention. For example you can say "wow, that's crazy, you gotta be kidding me, Janet said that? Unbelievable, I feel for you babe."

These expressions show to your wife that you are listening and you are there for her. Drop those short words every now and then to keep the conversation two ways and not boring. You really don't have to construct sentences.

Just try not to do this often. She might realize your trick and feel that you are not giving her attention.

At times you may not have energy to drop any word and you sense the conversation is something that can be postponed, ask her to defer the conversation till later. Immediately tell her the reason why you asked to defer it and I'm sure she will respect that you are tired. When it's later you are well rested, take the initiative to bring up the conversation. This shows that you take her serious and you have her in mind.

This situation goes both ways. When I'm the one who has something to share and my wife is tired, she will simply ask if we can defer the conversation till later when she has gained a little bit of energy. If the conversation is something that cannot be postponed, she will tell me she's listening but she cannot talk that much. This helps us to communicate effectively and avoid unnecessary arguments.

You may not know how women think and react to every situation but these two situations you can handle very well and help save arguments. Build her dressing time into your schedule and show verbal expressions to her while she discusses her concerns.

HE'S NOT INTERESTED

People get upset and emotionally depressed when they go on a date and nothing they expect comes out from it. At first he was attracted to you, he showed initial interest, called you to schedule the first date and after the date, he was nowhere to be found. What supposed to become the aftermath of the date, a call for second date ends up being no call back, no text, no second date, and opportunity to be in a relationship.

These are obvious signs that he's no longer interested in you. His perception of you prior to the date did not become his reality. He has discovered some things about you during the date or after the date that prohibit future date and consideration for relationship.

This happens vice-versa as well. Guys are hoping the first date will lead to second date. Thought a great connection was made, cracked jokes, ensured conversation was not boring, felt the right things were said at the right time, impressed her and took her to the nice restaurant. But those things were not considered to get you the second date.

There are many aspects of what makes someone qualified to be the ideal choice of partner. People just don't wake up and randomly select who they want to spend the rest of their lives with. There are processes and considerations that lead to down selecting choices to one.

In order to excel to the next date, you must first pass the first date and series of tests. Your date is more like a job interview. Before you get hired for a job, the employer schedules a face to face interview to go through your resume, your skills set, past work experiences, education background etc. If the employer likes your resume and how you are able to defend it, they will consider you for the position you applied for.

Same concept with relationship. Your objective is to be considered for a boyfriend or girlfriend position based on your experiences and skills acquisitions. The employer in this case is your date and will determine if you are best qualified based on your resume, which is basically what you say you are.

Resume has some essential areas but let's consider two important ones that your date will utilize to determine if you are a good fit.

Education: A man is looking at your level of education to determine how much money you can bring to the table, contribute to the family. The level of education determines how much money one can earn. All things equal, someone with an Associate degree will not be making more than someone with a Bachelor, Master degree or PhD.

The man makes a projection plan of his future. He wants to get married in next two years, he realizes all the finances will be on him since you are not making much as a result of you having an Associate degree. Let's say you are going to have a kid a year later after the wedding, most of the expenses will still fall on him. And when he asks about your future goals during the interview, you don't reply with anything about going back to school to get your Bachelor or master degree. That tells him you are not ambitious; you will become a liability and nothing to offer him. He decides in his mind you are not qualified to be his girlfriend and future wife.

Your level of education also suggests the level of your intelligence and knowledge. It can also make you and your partner either stand out in the crowd or not. If you and your partner are incompatible intellectually, it will be hard for communication to flow well. The conversation will be boring and awkward. You won't see eye to eye, it will be challenging to reason well together, and most likely, you will not be talking that much at home.

Does your degree make your partner look good in front of his friends, family? How would it feel when he's out among his friends who are Master degree holder, PhDs, Business exec, Senior level at work and you are only getting by with a two year degree and working at food lion, doing some blue collar job? The introduction of you to his friends won't go smoothly and you will not be relatable.

Employment History: The employer wants to see who you have worked for, what kind of work you did for them, and how long you worked with them. Likewise your date is also interested in who you have messed with, what type of activities you engaged with them, and how long you stayed in the relationship.

If you have been with six people in a matter of two years that means you were averaging one mate in every four months. While you may think this is not a bad record, sorry to burst your bubble, it is significantly a bad record to have.

Imagine placing that on your resume with an employer considering you for a position. They will not even hire you because your record shows no loyalty, longevity career with each company you worked for. They think you will jump ship soon if they hire you just like you did with other companies.

He thinks your commitment life span is short. If you couldn't keep a relationship with a person for two years, you won't possibly be with him for that long as well. Therefore, it will be a waste of time to have you as a partner.

Who you have being with also tells the kind of person you are! Assuming you worked for a few fortune 100 companies in the past, any other fortune 100 companies will love to hire you because they know you must be valuable and highly exceptional to have worked for fortune 100 companies.

Everyone is looking for that exceptional person to be with. One that is the right match, peculiar, and rare to have.

Not someone that is gullible and can be accessible by anybody.

BACKGROUND CHECK

The next thing an employer considers after examining your resume is background. I've heard so many sad stories of people passing interviews and then fail background check. Imagine going through tough interview, keeping nice resume and then one or two things the employer finds while conducting a background check blows the offer away. That will make someone lose his mind.

While conducting a background check, employer wants to examine your activities on social media, investigate if you have any criminal background, drug dealings, etc. This is also important to someone who wants to have you as a partner. He's finding out from friends or people that might know you to discover if you have done anything terrible and negative that could be repeated.

Then he takes it to social media to find out the pictures, videos, and status you are posting. Ladies, if you are always taking pictures with different guys, revealing your body, twerking, dancing on the pole, always partying, and drinking alcohol then the message you are sending about yourself will not get you a girlfriend seat with a guy who is looking for a decent, conservative, and classy lady.

If you are also bashing guys on social media, posting negative comments about them, it discourages potential man to approach you. To him, your messages suggest that you are not interested in being with a guy and he stands no chance with you because he's already being judged and categorized in your description of men. Don't let your past experience about men dictate that every man will be the same. Every man cannot be the same.

Always have something positive to say. Talk about news, current events, God, etc. Post pictures of you wearing nice outfits, smiling, going to church and more pictures of you going to church lol Men like godly women.

Having a good history and clean background will get you in a girlfriend seat and possibly make you a wife if you play your cards right. Make sure that your activity and engagements on social media are positive and reflect good lifestyle. In order not to be considered illiterate, liability, and experience boring conversations, get your Certifications, Bachelor, Master and/or PHD degree. If your partner is investing in himself and you are not, one day you will be incompatible.

QUESTIONS AND ANSWERS

Here are some of the questions I have come across and my perspectives and responses to them just in case you find yourself asking some of these questions.

(1) I am angry and frustrated at God because I am still unmarried in my late thirties.

Response:

God may not be the reason behind your frustration and if He is, then He has a good reason for it. Jeremiah 29:11 says: "For I know the plans I have for you, declares the LORD, plans to prosper you and not harm you, plans to give you hope and a future." God knows beginning from the end and end from the beginning. I'm sure he's aware of your situation and He can fix it for you if you go to Him humbly, ask Him to give you the understanding of the situation.

Practically, what are you doing to find a soul mate? Finding a soul mate entails many things such as having good character, working on yourself to attract and complement your desired partner. The sections of the book on Complement and Attraction: Transformational Approach to Dating went into details. By following the guides laid out in these sections, I'm positive you will meet your partner soon and get married.

People themselves also contribute to their own situations. We often times delay, making decisions due to personal reasons. In our early twenties, youthful days, we tend to play games. One of those women or men could have been a life partner. Once you recognize a marriage-material person, don't mess with his mind. Date and keep him.

(2) If we don't have sex before marriage, how can I tell that the man I want to marry is sexually capable and fertile?

Response

Spiritually, God does not honor sex before marriage as it is written in Hebrews 13:4: "Let marriage be held in honor among all, and let the marriage bed be undefiled, for God will judge the sexually immoral and adulterous." We are also living in an advanced society and science has improved over the years. You can consult a doctor and have the doctor conduct a fertility test for your wife and yourself if indeed you are concerned about the ability of giving birth. Having to test drive your wife like a car to buy is not the right approach. Women are human beings, not material things. If you test-drive her and she gets pregnant that will prove to you she is fertile. However, there are consequences to that.

First, having a child before marriage has nullified the chance of having a white wedding. Since the days women were young, they have always hoped for a white wedding: A beautiful long wedding gown with their friends behind them as bride's maids and all the ceremonies that come with such a glorious day. As a man, you don't want to ruin that for her, as she will remember it for the rest of her life.

Second, you can think of telling her to terminate the baby. But that shows you don't care for human life and the termination can go wrong to affect her chances of having another baby.

Thirdly, it is a shameful look when you have a baby before marriage. Her parents will not be happy with that condition. It is better to keep the marriage bed undefiled in order not to offend God and destroy what could have turned out to be a great wedding.

(3) Everyone I have prayed with and spoken to about my relationship, including my parents, does not support it. But I love my fiancé and I feel at peace when I think of our future together. What can I do?

Response

It is easy to convince one's self that the person you are with is the right one, especially when so much in love. Emotions are involved, you are head over heels, or age is no longer on your side. That is not to say you may not be right about your partner. However, God is the only one who can actually reveal to you that your partner is His right choice for you. When you go with God's choice, the opinions of people don't matter. This situation only requires you to hear from God directly and heed His opinion. Involve your fiancé to pray as well for her to get a confirmation. Everyone in this relationship needs to hear from God individually and be on the same page.

If God reveals that your partner is your soul mate, then the next step is to have your pastor, an elderly person in the family, or your parents' friends whom they respect talk to your parent. It is advisable to receive the blessings of your parents over your marriage. Marriage is a big deal and parents want their children to choose the right partners and live happily.

(4) Is it advisable to marry a brother who just relocated to the U.S from another country, with no solid means of income?

Response

I understand that you are worried about his financial status and if he's capable of taking care of the family. Marriage is like a car and money is the oil that keeps it going. Money is a major driver in marriage. Even the bible says in 1Timothy 5:8: "But if anyone does not provide for his own, and especially for those of his household, he has denied the faith and is worse than an unbeliever." God is interested in a husband being financially equipped and capable of providing for his family.

Due to the circumstances surrounding the brother, he might not be fit to provide in the way you expect, especially if he does not have the right credentials and documents to obtain a real job. It is advisable to marry the brother if he proves to be a good man in all other aspects, i.e., respect, moral, character, spiritual, etc. It takes time for people from another country to get acclimatize to the system in United State. Finding a descent job, getting his papers, and obtaining his driver's license might be taking longer than expected.

If you truly like this brother and he is the one whom God has chosen for you, then assist him in any way you can. We only see today, not tomorrow. His later days can be much better than his beginnings and I'm sure he will not forget the humble beginning and the assistance you offered. Consider whatever you do now as an investment into your family.

(5) I have been talking to a brother for five years and he is yet to propose. How long is too long to court?

Response

Traditionally, courtship is between two and three years. It is not to say you cannot take it further than that or cut it shorter for rational reasons. For example, some people might want to court longer because they are still in school and would like to be done or almost done before they take that relationship to the next level. It can also be that the person is still unsure if the partner is the right one.

The best thing to do is to have a discussion with your partner and find out what is delaying the relationship from progressing to the next phase. You don't want to be second-guessing or making excuses. Get to the bottom of it and have him be honest with his response. Five years is a long time and adequate enough to determine if you are the one or not. I offered the way to talk to the brother about this in the book section: Confusion of Women when Dating.

(6) I am a sister interested in a brother in church. But he is not showing interest. What should I do?

Response

You should not be the one first coming off and showing interest. The Bible says in Proverbs 18:22 that "He who finds a wife finds what is good and receives favor from the Lord." It is a man's job to find you, to show interest and it is your choice to accept him if you find him to be ideal. However, it happens occasionally that a man may not notice you in the crowd. He might actually be looking and not pay close attention to you. He might be engrossed with bills, school, and work.

If indeed you are interested in him, then reveal yourself to him and one of the ways to do that in church is to have a casual talk with him. Start a conversation by saying, "I don't see you at the young–adult meeting in church or some kind of group meeting." Say something that is applicable to both of you so that it doesn't feel obvious that you are showing interest in him.

(7) What are some of the red flags to look out for in a relationship, so I do not fall into error?

Response

It's good to be aware of a few red flags that elude the minds of the people when getting involved in a relationship. Red flags are signs that can build your confidence to determine whether the person is the right fit for you or not. Spiritual focus is always a good start. Double check that the person is a believer and equally yoked with you. Make sure he is not serving a different God from you.

Ensure he is not coming to church just because of you. Before they got married, a lady who was a Christian told the prospective husband who is a Muslim that he had to convert to Christianity before she could marry him. Because the man wanted to marry her, he went to church with her, showing that he was interested in becoming a Christian. Following their wedding, the husband went back to his Islamic religion. The husband only went to church those times to deceive her in order for them to get married.

Now the husband leaves the house Sunday morning to the mosque while the wife leaves to church. This has negatively impacted their children. The children are young and can't make decisions for themselves of what faith to follow. Each parent has a vested interest in what faith he or she wants their children to follow. That creates issues at least every Sunday morning. The husband wants the children to follow him to the mosque and likewise the wife wants the children to go with her to church. This situation also brought a dilemma of whether to give the children Christian names, Muslim names, or both. Being equally yoked is an important foundation to marriage.

A plethora of other red flags are anger, pride, and addiction to video games, alcohol, and cigarettes. These are major in a relationship. Also a person who has no self-control gets ticked off and can be physically, emotionally, and verbally abusive. When arguments occur and he can't manage to keep his cool, he tends to curse you, elevates to battering.

A proud individual may not listen to your advice. He feels lofty and thinks he knows it all, which can bring his own downfall. It's even critical if he is the one always making major decisions that impact the family. Marriage is a joint effort and everyone plays a role to build it up. Therefore no one should feel rebellious against one another. Ephesians 5:21 says, "Submit to one another out of reverence for Christ."

1 Peter 5:5 says, "Likewise, you who are younger, be subject to the elders. Clothe yourselves, all of you, with humility toward one another, for God opposes the proud but gives grace to the humble." Proverbs 22:4 says, "The reward of humility and the fear of Jehovah is riches, and honor, and life."

Women have complained about the addiction of men with video games. The time the man's supposed to spend with the wife, he's busy playing video games by himself or with his boys. It makes sense to have a "Me time or Personal space" in the family that can be used for playing video games. However, life requires balance and the ability to balance it well. Addiction is not a good thing. If you are a man who always gets yelled at by your partner about your addiction to video games and not making time for her, reduce your time spent playing the video games. You can also teach her how to play the video games so that you can both enjoy it together. That is spending time together.

Poor lifestyle choices of addiction to alcohol and cigarettes can send people to their graves early. It is not healthy to drink or smoke. The consequences weigh more than the pleasure people get from it. If you are looking for a serious partner, make sure your partner does not have any of these addictions because you don't want to get married and a few years later become a widow raising the whole family by yourself.

(8) Is it okay to contact my fiancé's ex to learn more about him/her?

Response

It is absolutely NOT okay to take such a step. Ex means old story, old news. The last thing you want to do is to bring the Ex into the picture. Doing that gives the Ex power and confidence that she knows more than you. Understand that you are the new sheriff in town. That means you need to learn about the town on your own, get to know the inhabitant, and make changes that are necessary to make the town peaceful. The opinion of the previous people who used to live in the town does not matter, especially if the town has now changed or needs to change.

It is your turn to build history together with your partner. Spiritually, you can go to God, and He will reveal hidden things about your partner. Daniel 2:22 says, "He reveals deep and hidden things; he knows what lies in darkness, and light dwells with him." God can tell you how to make your partner happy. My wife asks God different things she can do around the house to make me happy and God reveals them to her and she's stunned when I react happily to those things.

(9) A brother has been asking me out for lunch, he is a good guy, has a good job, is educated, and really loves God, but I honestly cannot get over the fact that he dresses poorly and has a slight body odor. He also has a huge ego, and I don't know how to tell him about these flaws without hurting him.

Response

A good way to start is by becoming his friend. We tend to listen to our friends more than a stranger or someone we are not yet familiar with. Reason being that we think our friends won't judge us and want the best for us. Once you have established the friendship, let him know what he needs to change. Another approach is to buy him cologne and a shirt for a special occasion or celebration, i.e., his birthday. Tell him you think the shirt will look good on him and cologne will bring out a new smell. Express to him you like this new look and smell on him. I'm sure he will get it that way.

(10) All the ladies I approach in church have rejected me. I love God, have a decent job, and decent looks, what do women really want?

Response

A few of them you have mentioned including a God-fearing man. A man who can lead the family in the right path and a man they can aspire to be. Women are also looking for a confident and witty man. It's good to be brilliant but women want to laugh and be entertained. No woman wants to be home bored with nothing to do. They don't want to be around a man who cannot make them laugh. The Bible says in the book of Proverbs 17:22: "A joyful heart is good medicine; but a broken spirit dries up the bones."

Since you have approached some ladies in the church, a simple practical step is to ask a few of those ladies why they rejected you. It's just like going for a job interview. If you didn't pass a few interviews, ask the interviewer why you were not chosen. The answers can be mind blowing and help you to land the next job. Even a better one than you had previously applied for.

Take a leap of faith and ask a few of the ladies why they rejected you. They may have similar reasons, which if you apply, can have those girls falling for you and eating out the palm of your hands. If not, the correction can actually bring about a girl who is even more beautiful and pleasant than those who rejected you. There is a lesson in challenges we go through. Find that lesson. It can help you overcome your next challenge.

Do you have a book that you would like to get published?

Get published for free at: www.lightswitchpress.com

Printed in Great Britain
by Amazon

55789663R00059